VIKINGS VS. HUNS

Disclaimer:

The battles in this book are not real. It is fun to imagine. These 2 opponents would never fight each other in real life.

45th Parallel Press

Published in the United States of America by Cherry Lake Publishing
Ann Arbor, Michigan
www.cherrylakepublishing.com

Reading Adviser: Marla Conn, MS, Ed., Literacy specialist, Read-Ability, Inc.
Book Designer: Melinda Millward

Photo Credits: © Fotokvadrat/Shutterstock.com, back cover, 10; © Khosrork/istock, cover, 5; © enkhtamir/istock, cover, 5; © lassedesignen/Shutterstock.com, 6; © Lorado/istock, 9, 29; © Fotokvadrat/Shutterstock.com, 10; ©Erik Peterson/Alamy Stock Photo, 12; © Rawpixel/istock, 15; ©Photo 12/Alamy Stock Photo, 16; © GraphicsRF/Shutterstock.com, 19, 20; © Nejron Photo/Shutterstock.com, 19; © vectortatu/Shutterstock.com, 20; © steve estvanik/Shutterstock.com, 21; © Khosro/Shutterstock.com, 23; © vadimmmus/Shutterstock.com, 24; © IAM photography/Shutterstock.com, 25; © Boltenkoff/Shutterstock.com, 25; © Reimar/Shutterstock.com, 27

Graphic Element Credits: © studiostoks/Shutterstock.com, back cover, multiple interior pages; © infostocker/Shutterstock.com, back cover, multiple interior pages; © mxbfilms/Shutterstock.com, front cover; © MF production/Shutterstock.com, front cover, multiple interior pages; © AldanNi/Shutterstock.com, front cover, multiple interior pages; © Andrii Symonenko/Shutterstock.com, front cover, multiple interior pages; © acidmit/Shutterstock.com, front cover, multiple interior pages; © manop/Shutterstock.com, multiple interior pages; © Lina Kalina/Shutterstock.com, multiple interior pages; © mejorana/Shutterstock.com, multiple interior pages; © NoraVector/Shutterstock.com, multiple interior pages; © Smirnov Viacheslav/Shutterstock.com, multiple interior pages; © Piotr Urakau/Shutterstock.com, multiple interior pages; © IMOGI graphics/Shutterstock.com, multiple interior pages; © jirawat phueksriphan/Shutterstock.com, multiple interior pages

45th Parallel Press is an imprint of Cherry Lake Publishing.

Library of Congress Cataloging-in-Publication Data

Names: Loh-Hagan, Virginia, author.
Title: Vikings vs. Huns / by Virginia Loh-Hagan.
Other titles: Vikings versus Huns
Description: [Ann Arbor] : [Cherry Lake Publishing], [2019] | Series: Battle royale : lethal warriors | Audience: Grades: 4-6. | Includes bibliographical references and index.
Identifiers: LCCN 2019003648| ISBN 9781534147652 (hardcover) | ISBN 9781534150515 (pbk.) | ISBN 9781534149083 (pdf) | ISBN 9781534151949 (hosted ebook)
Subjects: LCSH: Vikings—Warfare—Juvenile literature. | Huns—Warfare—Juvenile literature. | Imaginary wars and battles—Juvenile literature.
Classification: LCC DL66 .L64 2019 | DDC 948/.022—dc23
LC record available at https://lccn.loc.gov/2019003648

Printed in the United States of America
Corporate Graphics

About the Author

Dr. Virginia Loh-Hagan is an author, university professor, former classroom teacher, and curriculum designer. She has written books about Norse gods and goddesses. She lives in San Diego with her very tall husband and very naughty dogs. To learn more about her, visit www.virginialoh.com.

Table of Contents

Introduction

Imagine a battle between Vikings and Huns. Who would win? Who would lose?

Enter the world of *Battle Royale: Lethal* **Warriors**! Warriors are fighters. This is a fight to the death! The last team standing is the **victor**! Victors are winners. They get to live.

Opponents are fighters who compete against each other. They challenge each other. They fight with everything they've got. They use weapons. They use their special skills. They use their powers.

They're not fighting for prizes. They're not fighting for honor. They're not fighting for their countries. They're fighting for their lives. Victory is their only option.

Let the games begin!

In real life, nobody really wins in a war.

VIKINGS

Vikings came from areas around Norway, Sweden, Denmark, and Iceland.

People fled when they saw Viking ships enter their waters. Vikings were Norse seamen. They were fierce. They raided across Europe. But their main enemies were the British. The Vikings sailed. They landed. They attacked. They took people as slaves. They stole from churches. They burned buildings. They took anything they wanted.

They were explorers. They took over many kingdoms. They discovered the Americas long before Christopher Columbus. They were also known to travel to Russia.

They were traders. They made beautiful metal and wood things. They used these things to buy silver, spices, and other things. The Viking Age was during the 8th to 11th centuries. They ruled the seas at that time.

Vikings had their own honor code. They attacked anyone who shamed them. They weren't afraid to die. This made them fearless.

They had powerful ships. Their ships could fit many people. They could travel in hard places. They could travel for a long time. They were designed for quick landings and escapes.

Vikings sailed with many ships. They rammed into enemy ships. They boarded these ships. They took control. They **looted**. Loot is to rob.

They were also good fighters on land. They fought with shields. They fought with swords. They fought with axes. They fought with spears. They fought with **battering rams**. These are poles that ram into buildings.

All Viking males were required to own weapons. They carried them at all times.

Some Vikings were called berserkers. **Berserk** means to go crazy. They wore bearskins. They hit fast. They hit hard. They ignored pain. They lacked control. They kept fighting no matter what. They were scary.

Vikings didn't fight in **formation**. Formations are when soldiers march in rows. Vikings didn't follow orders. They did what needed to be done. They were loyal to each other. They had the same goals. Their fighting style focused on the moment.

Vikings depended on their sea skills. They attacked from sea. So, many cities built walls and forts. They protected themselves from Vikings. Vikings were less likely to fight those cities.

FUN FACTS ABOUT VIKINGS

- Vikings didn't call themselves Vikings. They called themselves Norse, Norsemen, or Danes. Viking means "pirate." It comes from the Old Norse language.
- Funerals honor the dead. Vikings put the dead body in a small boat. They put in clothes, animals, and jewelry. They set the boat on fire. They pushed it out to sea.
- Vikings admired strong people. They were known to leave behind sick children. They'd leave them in the wild. They'd also throw them into the sea.
- Vikings wanted to be blonde. They used a strong soap to wash their hair. The soap bleached their hair.
- Vikings are known as fighters. But they spent most of their time farming.
- Vikings bathed more than other Europeans. They washed at least once a week. They invented the combs we use today. They also made tweezers. They made razors. They made ear spoons to scoop out wax.

HUNS

Huns were also called barbarians.

Huns struck fear in the hearts of many. They were a group of **nomadic** tribes. Nomads move from place to place. Tribes are groups. Huns lived in the **steppes** of central Asia. Steppes are dry, grassy plains. Huns hunted. They gathered. They lived off the land.

Huns were most powerful in the 5th century. They were raiders. They raided much of Europe. Their main enemies were the Romans. Huns destroyed cities. They invaded. They attacked. They looted. They made people pay them for safety. (They were like the mob.)

Huns didn't really fight for riches. (Of course, they liked being rich.) But they fought because they liked fighting.

Huns were expert horse riders. They used their horses in battle. They moved quickly. Their horses were special. They were fast. They could travel long distances.

They were expert **archers**. Archers shoot bows and arrows. Huns were able to shoot while on their horses. They could hit men from far away. They hardly ever missed. They also used ropes. They roped enemies. They dragged them while on horseback.

They tricked their enemies. They didn't ride into their opponents. They rode around them. They'd shoot as they moved. They trained for war. They practiced military moves. They planned surprise attacks. They cut off their enemies' supplies.

Huns dressed simply. But they dressed their horses in gold, silver, and other gems.

Huns' main strength was their horses. But it was also their weakness. They spent all their time on horses. Their legs were a little weak. Huns weren't as strong on foot. Some stories say they walk clumsily.

Huns relied on fear to defeat their enemies. Stories of the Huns painted them as brutal fighters. Many cities **surrendered**. Surrender means to give up. These cities didn't want to fight the Huns. But this fear ended when Attila the Hun died. Attila was their leader. Lack of leadership made the Huns weak. When Attila died, their power ended. Huns' armies became weak.

FUN FACTS ABOUT HUNS

- Huns did everything on their horses. They slept on their horses. They even had parties while on horses.
- Huns didn't like hair on their faces. So, they burned hair off with fire. Or they cut off the hair with a knife. This made scars on their cheeks.
- Babies' heads are still growing. Theirs skulls aren't hard yet. Huns tightly wrapped their babies' heads. They changed the shape of their heads. They wanted heads to be longer.
- Huns slashed male babies' cheeks. This was done with a sword. This was done on the day the baby was born. The purpose was to make males endure pain.
- Huns didn't leave any written records. What we know about them comes from their enemies' records.
- Some believe China built the Great Wall of China to keep the Huns out.

CHOOSE YOUR BATTLEGROUND

Vikings and Huns are fierce fighters. They're well-matched. They like to raid. They destroy buildings. They **sack** towns. Sack means to loot and destroy. Vikings and Huns take things. They fight for land. They fight for control. They kill people. They're born to fight. But they have different ways of fighting. So, choose your battleground carefully!

Battleground #1: Sea

- Vikings are sailors. They live by the sea. They know how to build ships. They know how to sail. They can find their way around. They would easily win a sea battle.
- Huns are **landlocked**. This means they live far from the sea. Huns could fight on ships. But they'd have a hard time sailing.

Both Vikings and Huns were considered outsiders to Europeans.

Battleground #2: Land

- Vikings and Huns are both good land fighters. They can fight on solid ground. But Huns would win with their horses.

- Vikings are from the northern lands. They know how to fight in cold weather. Huns are from central Asia. They know how to fight in hot weather.

- Huns like to use the land. They set up surprise attacks. They set up guards to watch. Vikings like to attack a targeted area.

Battleground #3: Mountains

- Vikings like to run back to their ships. If they're on a mountain, their ships would be far away.

- Huns aren't climbers. They aren't as strong without their horses. They'd have a hard time getting horses up mountains.

ARMED AND DANGEROUS: WEAPONS

Vikings: The most popular Viking weapon was the battle-axe. These axes were made for war. They had long handles. They had sharp blades at the end. They were light. They were fast. Vikings swung these axes. They could also throw them. Some axes had a lower blade. They could pull down opponents' shields. Some axes were so powerful that 2 Vikings were needed to hold them.

Huns: The most popular Hun weapon was the Hun bow. The bows were made from a special mixture. The Huns combined wood, sinew, horn, and bone. Sinew is tough tissue that holds muscles and bones together. The Huns used fish bladder to hold everything together. This mixture allowed the bow to curve back. This meant arrows could fly faster. They could hit targets at 100 yards (91 meters). These bows were also smaller and lighter than other bows. This made them easier to use on horseback.

FIGHT ON!

The battle begins! Ships land. Vikings come out hollering. They have shields in one hand. They have swords or axes in the other hand. Huns ride out with their horses. They're holding bows and arrows. They also have swords and spears on their belts.

Move 1:

All the Vikings rush to battle. They start swinging away. They slash anyone in their path. They even cut other Vikings. They're spread out all over the beach. Half the Huns ride out on their horses. The other half stay back. They guard the rest of the horses.

Vikings have horses as well. But their horses are smaller.

Move 2:

Huns shoot arrows at Vikings. Vikings use their shields. Huns aim for their legs. They quickly circle the Vikings. They trap them in the center. They use their spears to stab Vikings.

Move 3:

Some spears get stuck in the Vikings' shields. This gives Vikings time to swing at Huns. Their swords have blades on both sides. This means they cut in all directions. Huns keep moving on their horses. They want to confuse Vikings.

Vikings and Huns liked to ambush their enemies. Ambush means to trap or surprise.

LIFE SOURCE: FOOD FOR BATTLE

Vikings: Viking warriors spent a lot of time on ships. So they ate a lot of fish. A popular dish was hakarl. Hakarl is rotten shark. Vikings would catch a Greenland shark. This shark is poisonous when eaten fresh. Vikings cut off its head. They put it in a hole. They covered it with sand and dirt. They let it rot. They took it out. They hung it to dry. They waited for a brown crust to form. Then, they cut it into bits to be eaten.

Huns: Hun warriors ate foods with a lot of fat and that didn't need to be cooked. They were known to eat a special type of meat. They put it between their saddle and their horse. Saddles are seats on a horse. They rode all day. The meat got pounded. It became soft. The horse's sweat got mixed into the meat. This is like salt. It made the meat taste better. It also made it into a jerky.

Move 4:

Vikings make a shield wall. They all put up their shields. They defend against the Huns' attacks. They throw out spears. They start moving out of the center. They break through the horses.

Move 5:

This team of Huns **retreats**. Retreat means to go back. Vikings think they have quit. But Huns are just resting their horses. As they leave, they turn on their saddles. Huns keep shooting arrows. Meanwhile, the other team of Huns rushes out. They also shoot arrows at Vikings.

Move 6:

Vikings talk to each other. They plan as they fight. They break up into small groups. Each group has specific goals. They attack Huns in smaller groups.

Move 7:

Huns dash in and out. They attack. Then, they run away. They go back. They attack again.

Huns made their saddles in a special way. They could twist and turn.

AND THE VICTOR IS . . .

What are their next moves?
Who do you think would win?

Vikings could win if:

- They get Huns off their horses.
- They get rid of the horses. Huns change horses. They don't want to tire the horses. That way they can keep fighting.
- They get Huns to fight in close combat. Huns are expert archers. Vikings are better swordsmen.
- They kill Attila the Hun. Huns need Attila's leadership.

Huns could win if:

- They get rid of Vikings' ships. Vikings use their ships to escape. They use their ships to attack.
- They stay away from the sea. Vikings are expert sailors. They grew up by the sea.
- They get rid of the Vikings' weapons.

Both Vikings and Huns need a strong leader to last.

Vikings: Top Champion

Erik the Red was born in Norway. He had red hair. He had a red beard. He also had a red-hot temper. Murder ran in his family. His father had killed someone when Erik was age 10. His family had to leave Norway. They escaped to Iceland. Erik was tough. He was violent. He was quick to fight. In Iceland, men killed Erik's slaves. Erik got mad. He wanted revenge. Revenge is to get even. Erik killed the men. He was banished. He moved to another town. Around the year 982, Erik got in a fight with a neighbor. He killed 2 of his opponent's sons. He was banished again. This time, he sailed west. He went to a land he called Greenland. He said, "People would be attracted to go there if it had a favorable name." Later, he brought people to settle there. Stories say he died from falling off a horse.

Huns: Top Champion

Attila the Hun loved power. He killed his brother to become the sole ruler of the Huns. He was good to his own people. But he was cruel to others. He was known as the Scourge of God. Scourge means a whip used to punish. Attila led many invasions. He grew his empire. He destroyed lands. He took people as slaves. He said he owned the sword of Mars. Mars was the Roman god of war. Attila liked inspiring fear. He said, “There, where I have passed, the grass will never grow again.” He had several wives. His last marriage was in the year 453. He died on his wedding night. His nose bled. He choked on his own blood. His army cut their faces. They smeared their faces with blood. They rode horses around his body. His body was buried with riches. The servants who buried him were killed. No one knows where he’s buried.

Consider This!

THINK ABOUT IT!

- How are the Vikings and Huns alike? How are they different? Are they more alike or different? Why do you think so?
- If the Vikings and Huns lived at the same time, do you think they would've fought each other? If they did, who would've won? Why do you think so?
- Both the Vikings and Huns were fighters. They fought for more land. They fought for more resources. Learn more about their homelands. How did their homelands influence their fighting natures?
- Vikings are known for their Norse gods. Did the Huns have gods? If not, why not? If so, what are they like?
- Read the 45th Parallel Press book about Genghis Khan. If Genghis Khan and Attila the Hun fought, who would win? Why do you think so?

LEARN MORE!

- Higgins, Nadia. *Everything Vikings*. Washington, DC: National Geographic Children's Books, 2015.
- Kroll, Steven, and Robert Byrd (illust.). *Barbarians!* New York, NY: Dutton Children's Book, 2009.
- Margeson, Susan. *Viking*. New York, NY: DK Publishing, 2010.
- Price, Sean Stewart. *Attila the Hun: Leader of the Barbarian Hordes*. New York, NY: Franklin Watts, 2016.

GLOSSARY

archers (AHR-churz) people who shoot bows and arrows
battering rams (BAT-ur-ing RAMZ) big, heavy poles that are used to ram into doors and buildings
berserk (bur-ZURK) to go crazy
formation (for-MAY-shuhn) a formal arrangement used in military strategies
landlocked (LAND-lahkt) living in a place surrounded by land far away from the sea
looted (LOOT-id) stole; robbed
nomadic (noh-MAD-ik) moving from place to place
opponents (uh-POH-nuhnts) groups who compete against each other
retreats (rih-TREETS) to give up in a conflict
sack (SAK) to loot and destroy
saddles (SAD-uhlz) special seats used for riding horses
steppes (STEPS) dry, grassy plains
surrendered (suh-REN-durd) quit
victor (VIK-tur) the winner
warriors (WOR-ee-urz) fighters

INDEX